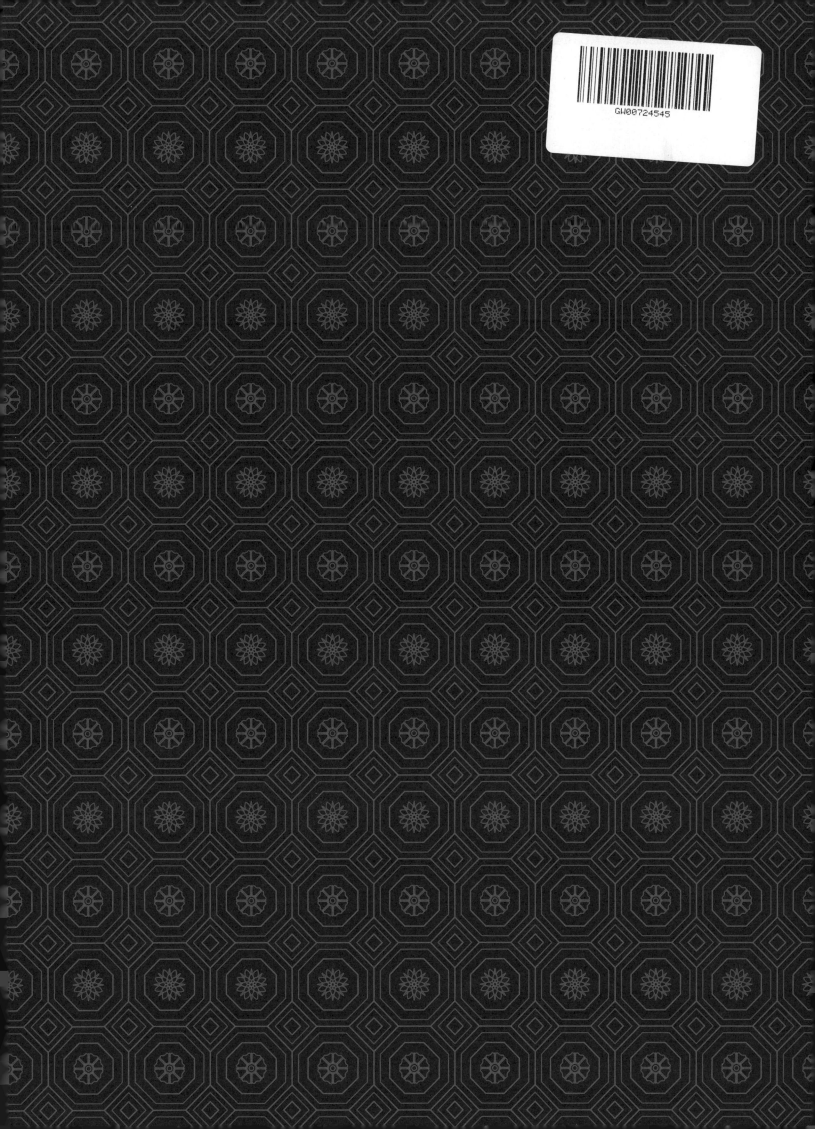

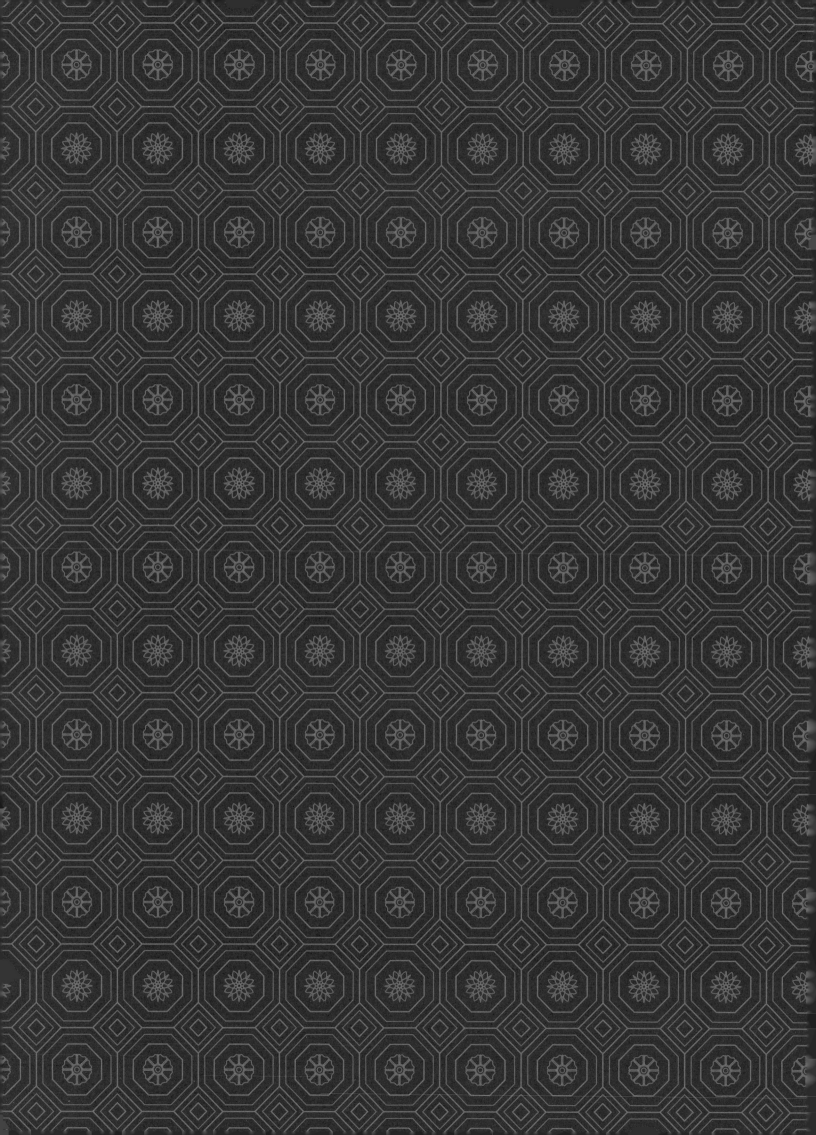

THE PENINSULA

LONDON

Text by Catherine Shaw

THE PENINSULA

L O N D O N

ASSOULINE

Oxford Street

Mayfair

Hyde Park

Serpentine Gallery

The Peninsula London

Consta

Grosvenor

Royal Albert Hall

Knightsbridge

Harrods

Sloane Street

Belgravia

Elizabeth Street

Victoria & Albert Museum

Sloane Square

Pavilion Road

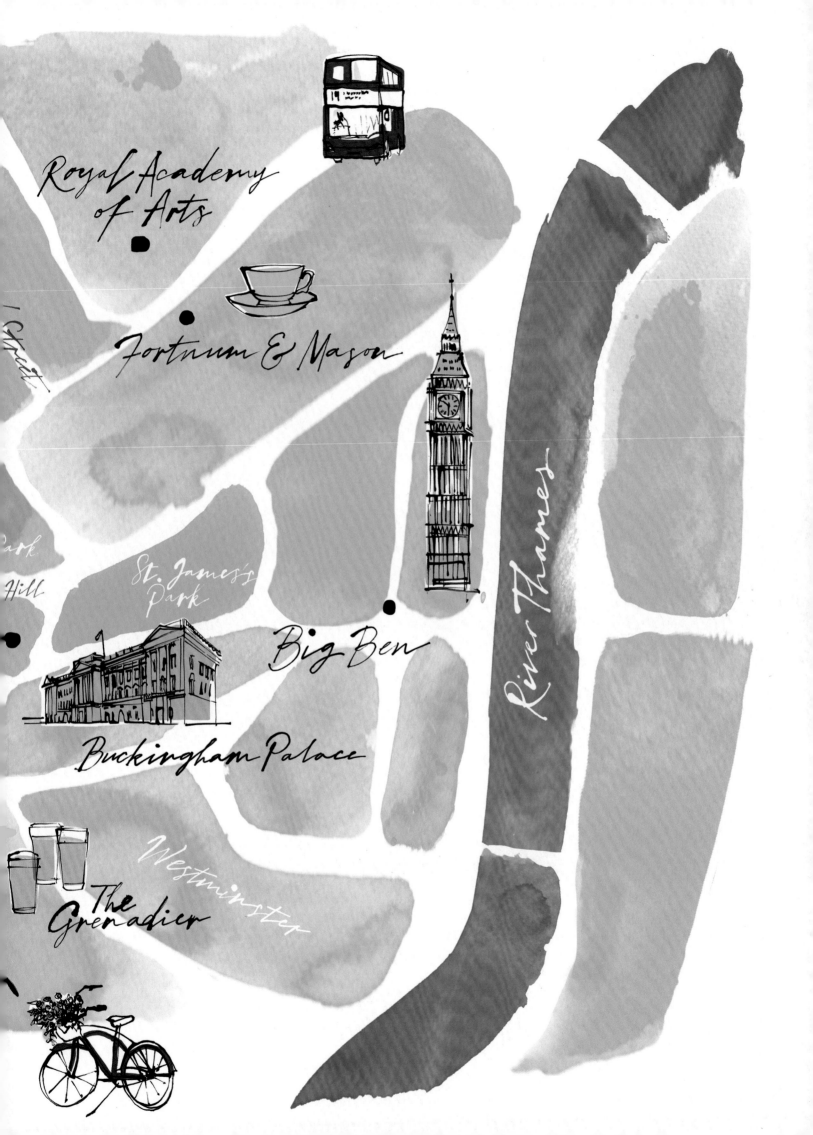

Royal Academy
of Arts

Fortnum & Mason

1 Street

Park
Hill

St. James's
Park

Big Ben

River Thames

Buckingham Palace

Westminster

The
Grenadier

Clockwise from top left: The Kadoorie family at The Peninsula London's Topping Out ceremony in 2019; Sir Elly Kadoorie with his sons Lawrence and Horace, c. 1920s; The Hon. Sir Michael Kadoorie at The Peninsula London; Sir Michael at Marble Hall, the Kadoorie family's Shanghai home, c. 1940s. *Following pages:* Illustration of the Royal Household Cavalry going through Wellington Arch in front of The Peninsula London. *Pages 12-13:* The hotel's elegant façade of Portland stone and Welsh slate.

Foreword

Every new Peninsula hotel opening brings a new sense of anticipation and new beginnings. In many ways, we are welcoming a new family member. The Peninsula London, our twelfth Peninsula hotel, holds a particularly special place in my heart.

Our company's heritage dates to 1866, and while we have often had to overcome great difficulties to achieve success, we have always looked ahead with optimism and confidence. As a result, we emerged as one of the leading hotel companies in the world, dedicated to serving our guests with the highest standards of luxury and warm hospitality.

The Hongkong and Shanghai Hotels have had numerous historical ties and connections to London, including Kadoorie family ties. My grandmother Laura Mocatta was born in London. My grandfather Sir Elly Kadoorie was knighted in the 1926 birthday honours for his services to charity and became a British citizen the following year. In 1981, my father, Lord Lawrence Kadoorie, was the first Hong Kong resident to be elevated to the peerage.

From the company's earliest days in 1866, we have sown deep roots between the United Kingdom and Hong Kong. We brought a general manager from London to run the first Hong Kong Hotel in 1868, and when the first Peninsula Hotel opened in Hong Kong in 1928 and became known as the "finest hotel east of Suez," we brought British traditions such as afternoon tea and tea dances to the Far East, and these remain Peninsula signatures today.

London has always been a "home away from home" for me. It is one of the world's great cosmopolitan and dynamic cities, and it is an exciting addition to our global family of hotels. In these pages you will read about the length of time it took to find exactly the right location for The Peninsula London, thirty-five years, as well as the unique challenges and difficult circumstances leading up to this hotel's opening during the pandemic years. This is a story of vision, perseverance, and more than a dash of courage. These values truly reflect the spirit of our company.

I would like to pay special tribute to our Chief Executive Officer, Clement Kwok, and Chief Operating Officer, Peter Borer, for their vision in bringing this hotel to life. I would also like to recognise every member of the team who was involved in building this hotel, and each of our committed staff members, who are offering the best standards of hospitality on a daily basis to our guests in London. You will meet many of these extraordinary characters in this book.

After so many decades of searching, and eventually finding such a perfect location in the very heart of Belgravia, I am delighted to introduce The Peninsula London to the world. Visit us, explore this magnificent hotel, enjoy the spectacular views, the delicious cuisine, and the unique Peninsula service, which we are renowned for around the world. It is my hope that this hotel becomes part of the fabric of London. Our international guests are vital, but the tapestry we walk on is a local tapestry, and our local community is always vital to our success.

I hope you enjoy the journey through this book and your own journey to The Peninsula London. It's a hotel, and a story, that I hope many people will wish to return to.

The Hon. Sir Michael Kadoorie
Chairman, The Hongkong and Shanghai Hotels, Limited

On Arrival

Traveller, imagine this hotel is a book.
Check in and stroll through its first chapter,
from the grand entrance's capital letter
to the last full stop of thought before sleep
on a pillow fluffed with clouds or dreams.

Today it might be a classic novel: a guest
arrives in the opening lines—a person like you
with zip codes and provinces trailing behind—
then heads for the sky in a hot air balloon to watch
the city's sundial unwinding the hours,
green shadows lounging in gardens and great parks.
To see famous landmarks trysting with great oaks.

Or let's say the hotel is a poem, each canto
a careful arrangement of china cups balanced
on china cups, a poem conjuring time and space
beyond the counties and cantons of home;
stone lions nod to let visitors pass
and two trees in the courtyard hold hands
maple to maple, leaf to leaf. In the rooftop bar
they serve lemon sestinas and neat villanelles...

Kick back, step out of those hot shoes
and wave hello in the framed mirror.
The pages are turning now and you're ready
to read the next scene or write the next verse
or stand at the window and drift out
into the view. Traveller, the story is you.

—*Poet Laureate Simon Armitage*

Your Story

In the words of the Poet Laureate, "Traveller, the story is you." Turn the pages.

This is a story of vision, perseverance, extraordinary individuals, and love.

This is London at its most elegant and charming, a delight for all the senses. Step into a world of warm Peninsula hospitality, an oasis from the relentless pace of the city outside, where wanderers from distant places immediately feel welcome and locals feel at home.

Pause for a moment and listen to the magnificent rhythmic trot of the Household Cavalry as they pass the hotel each morning; touch the smooth Portland stone; greet the majestic marble lions standing guard, protecting all who enter. Look across the leafy treetops of Royal Parks and palace gardens. Breathe in the crisp air, filled with light. London offers endless possibilities.

Note the beauty of the architecture, a fitting tribute to the grandeur of the Belgravia neighbourhood, and although new, it somehow feels as though it has always been there. Less tangible, but ever-present inside the hotel, are the love and precision that have gone into the tiniest detail created by local artisans and craftsmen at the pinnacle of their trade. All of this overseen by a team of dedicated staff, who truly understand and care deeply about the meaning of luxury and service.

Here, you can indulge your taste buds with delectable local cuisine, enhanced by delicate English bubbles in crystal glasses and hot tea served in bone-china cups. Feast your eyes upon hand-painted de Gournay murals depicting scenes of nearby Hyde Park, and idyllic landscapes painted by artists from the Royal Drawing School.

Those seeking a comfortable respite from the whirlwind pace of London will find it quietly waiting in the opulent suites and guest rooms, nestled in mahogany-panelled dressing rooms and large onyx bathrooms. Panoramic windows bathe the room in light, offering a silent vantage point over the busy city beneath.

This is an adventure story.

Intrepid travellers seeking indulgence and exhilaration will not have to look far. The golden era of British motorsports and aviation has been brought back to life; nostalgic MACH III cocktails, waiting to be sipped, fuel the experience below the graceful contours of the Concorde and the glittering city skyline beyond.

No mention of adventure could be made in these pages without paying respect to our heritage. A young man full of vitality and dreams, Elly Kadoorie set out from Baghdad in 1880, aspiring to make his fortune in the Far East. His third- and fourth-generation descendants—Sir Michael and his son Philip—have that same pioneering blood running through their veins. After their decades-long search, their legacy has come back to London, where the family also has roots.

This is a journey from East to West.

Within these walls, hospitality transcends barriers. Diplomacy reigns supreme. British traditions meld with Asian flair and ancient wisdom, a spice-trade fusion creating a family tradition of hospitality that will stand the test of time, welcoming future generations of visitors.

This is the story of The Peninsula London. Turn the pages and write the next verse.

Introduction

The Peninsula tale is one of a family with hospitality in its blood. It begins with Eleazer "Elly" Silas Kadoorie. Baghdad-born and a naturalised British citizen, Kadoorie married Laura Mocatta, whose family had lived in London since the sixteenth century. The couple went on to make Hong Kong, Shanghai, and London their homes. In 1890, Elly bought twenty-five shares in The Hongkong Hotel Company, as it was known then, and thus began the family's involvement and shareholding, which continue today.

Knighted in 1926, Sir Elly and his brother Ellis, along with Elly's sons, Lawrence and Horace, transformed Hong Kong's hospitality industry when, in 1928, they opened what was to become the Grande Dame and one of the most famous hotels in the world: The Peninsula Hong Kong.

The Peninsula Hong Kong represents the pinnacle of luxury, as does The Peninsula London. Hailed as a triumph of twentieth-century hospitality, architecture, and design, it quickly became *the* destination, drawing stylish passengers disembarking from ocean liners on the Tsim Sha Tsui waterfront, or arriving from Europe on the elegant Trans-Siberian Railway. Hong Kong high society flocked to The Lobby for cocktails and afternoon tea, to attend concerts and dinner dances that would become legendary, to celebrate special occasions, and to shop in the elegant fashion arcade that rivalled those of Paris. Everyone came, because the hotel represented what was exciting and alluring about Hong Kong, delivered with a flourish of East-meets-West that would eventually become a hallmark of The Peninsula Hotels worldwide.

Today, under the stewardship of Sir Michael Kadoorie, the Chairman of The Hongkong and Shanghai Hotels, his son Philip now by his side, the family's distinctive tradition of hospitality has expanded to eleven other properties across the world, from New York to Beverly Hills, Tokyo to Shanghai, from Paris to Istanbul, each celebrating the rich history and urban landscape of its locale while always adhering to the philosophy of the founders.

The Peninsula London marks the current chapter in this story. Hong Kong is the flagship, yet London has always held a special place in Sir Michael's heart, for his earliest memories are of visiting his Uncle Horace at his home in Knightsbridge. He always dreamed of a majestic hotel in London that would embody the soul of the city, and when it was his turn to take the reins of the family business, and because only the best site would do, he spent thirty-five years searching for the ideal London location, until eventually finding it in this exceptional city block on the edge of Belgravia overlooking Hyde Park Corner. What has been achieved is one of the most complex new builds ever undertaken in London, driven by a passionate team of individuals.

Top row, from left: The flagship hotel, The Peninsula Hong Kong, opened in 1928; The Peninsula Hotels' fleet of automobiles are finished in Brewster Green. *Middle row:* A tea dance at The Peninsula Hong Kong, c. 1930; The Lobby of The Peninsula Hong Kong, c. 1950. *Bottom row:* Chief Operating Officer Peter Borer (left) and Chief Executive Officer Clement Kwok (right) pictured at The Peninsula London's opening-day ceremony; The Peninsula's long association with luxury carmaker Rolls-Royce was famously mentioned in the 1974 James Bond film, *The Man with the Golden Gun.*

It has become the canvas for Sir Michael's plan to create a hotel where British heritage and elegance match the impeccable service of the East. A hotel designed to last for centuries as a personal legacy and testament to the city of London. And, as the Poet Laureate says so eloquently, it is where you, the guest, are always at the very heart of the story, a story set in the royal neighbourhood of Belgravia, where modern life and ancient traditions mingle freely with stately Georgian and Victorian architecture, gardens, squares, and parks.

Before The Peninsula London could come to fruition, the unassuming post-war office buildings occupying the site had to be removed, and taking care not to disturb nearby residents, the builders introduced sophisticated techniques to manage the inevitable vibrations, noise, and dust. The construction of the new building, designed by pre-eminent British firm Hopkins Architects, set a new benchmark in addressing neighbourhood sensitivities as far as disruption was concerned.

As he has done with multiple other new Peninsula hotels around the world, Peter Borer, the company's Chief Operating Officer, led a dizzying array of players, guiding designers and builders. At one point there were about 1,600 people working on-site, and a large part of the process was undertaken during the unique constraints of the global pandemic that broke out in 2020. During the early design stage, delicate negotiations continued to allow for the important fine-tuning of the architectural design. Just as Italian architecture had previously inspired Belgravia, The Peninsula London was conceived as a palazzo whose symmetrical frontage sits above a colonnade onto the public realm. The height of the building was maximised by stepping back the sixth, seventh, and eighth floors in glass and Welsh slate so that they read as an attic storey. A beautifully designed separate street entrance was created for the Chinese restaurant Canton Blue and its adjacent bar Little Blue, and The Peninsula Boutique & Café was added—along with enticing outdoor seating, which has since become a popular neighbourhood meeting spot.

As the signature of The Peninsula brand is meticulous attention to quality, full-size replica model rooms were built, allowing the team to design and evaluate every detail at scale. Multiple plywood options were also fabricated in Hong Kong, with a final room constructed on-site in London to act as the standard for the construction and fit-out teams. No improvement was too much to consider. Recalling an early visit to the site, Mike Taylor and Jim Greaves of Hopkins Architects said, "We were standing where the lobby would be built, and at that moment we saw the Household Cavalry go past on horseback. Peter Borer said, 'I love that. That's what our guests want. They want to know they're in London.' That conversation was the start of a discussion on how to best position the entrance, which led to us raising the lobby floor several feet above ground level to deliver a sense of theatre."

The Peninsula London's position in the very heart of the capital is singular. Great care was taken to ensure the design of the façade integrated seamlessly into the distinguished streetscape of dignified town houses, with their historic white stucco façades, intricate cornices, pilasters, and wrought-iron balconies. Extensive studies of the neighbourhood and close engagement with Historic England and the Westminster authorities meant that when the hotel opened in September 2023, Sir Michael could observe, "It feels in many ways as if

Clockwise from top left: Peter Borer, Chief Operating Officer of The Hongkong and Shanghai Hotels; architectural drawing by Hopkins Architects illustrating the hotel's Italian-palazzo-inspired façade; Peninsula Pages wearing their distinctive white uniform and pillbox hat in front of Wellington Arch during the The Peninsula London's construction. *Following pages:* The Household Cavalry in front of the hotel going through Wellington Arch on their way to the Changing of the Guard.

The "London Peninsula Cocktail"

2/3 PETER MARINO MODERN 1/3 ENGLISH HERITAGE 1 OLIVE EXOTIC ASIAN / MIDDLE EASTERN

May 2014

THE PENINSULA
LONDON

The Peninsula London has always been there, acting as a gateway to Belgravia." The wider heritage landscape includes the three Royal Parks, and this is mirrored in the hotel's courtyard, by master landscape architect Enzo Enea, with delicate climbing wisteria and a stately pair of 120-year-old Japanese maples at its centre.

Behind the hotel's Portland-stone frontage, renowned architect and designer of interiors Peter Marino has created spaces that radiate a quiet sophisticated luxury through sumptuous materials and an emphasis on symmetry and proportion. Every corner reflects the serious consideration that is the hallmark of the property. Marino drew inspiration for the aesthetic concept of the hotel from the perfect proportions of a classic martini. At an early meeting with Sir Michael, he sketched one to illustrate just how it is structured on the golden ratio based on the perfect botanical balance of two ingredients and a garnish—his contemporary conceptualisation of the hotel, founded on the spirit of London, with a refreshing twist of the East. "It's two-thirds me, one-third English Heritage—and then, having read the story of Sir Michael's family moving from the Middle East to China in the 1880s, I thought of this exotic aspect as the olive in the martini," Marino explains.

His vision for the hotel blends modernity with timeless elegance. Large windows frame breathtaking views of the city and parks, and the interiors emanate a sense of calm and harmony, creating a sanctuary of space and natural light. Indeed, Britain's natural landscape is a delicate theme that runs throughout the interiors, including the 190 guest rooms and suites—among the largest in London—furnished with pieces designed by Marino to pay homage to the capital with a fresh take on the original Peninsula design philosophy.

The same care was extended to the design of the private residences, the last of their kind to be built in Westminster since new planning regulations capped applications at a far smaller size. One- to five-bedroom apartments with floor-to-ceiling windows and spectacular views are tucked away in a private wing with its own entrance, a Peter Marino-designed twenty-five-metre pool, a gymnasium, and spa treatment rooms, in addition to discreet direct access to the hotel and to a private screening room.

And when it comes to entertaining or special occasions, the hotel's two ballrooms conjure up a stately Belgravia residence with refined gold textures, timber joinery, Bohemian glass wainscoting, and woven wall panels. There are soaring coffered ceilings with sparkling chandeliers too and, in a nod to idiosyncratic British style, an opulent animal-print carpet, and an elevator large enough to accommodate a car. Marino says that when he designs, he thinks about how people might feel as they enter and move through a space. "The most important thing is how it makes them feel," he explains. "You always have an emotional response to the interiors of a building. It's a little bit like us—we all have rich inner lives."

Over the past century the essential elements of Peninsula signature style have been distilled in a combination of Asian hospitality, meticulous service, and gracious staff dedicated to the fine art of anticipating a guest's needs. In London, the dialogue between East and West begins in the courtyard, where two Japanese maple trees stand together—"leaf to leaf"—an ancient Oriental symbol of longevity. At the

Top row, from left: A stone lion at the hotel's entrance was carved from a single piece of Han white marble; the bespoke hand-painted de Gournay mural in The Lobby depicts scenes of Hyde Park; The Lobby's decorative coffered ceiling. *Middle row:* The Peninsula London's distinctive Brewster Green livery; hand-drawn sketch by Peter Marino illustrating his design concept; Peninsula Pages are emblematic of The Peninsula's personal service. *Bottom row:* The Peninsula Residences London swimming pool; The Ballroom lobby features mosaic artwork by Ben Jakober and Yannick Vu; the Peter Marino-designed marble inlay floor in The Lobby.

entrance, Peninsula Pages, impeccable in their immaculate white suits, are ready with a cheerful "Welcome to The Peninsula London!" They whisk you inside, past the pair of stone lions, each carved by master artisans in northern China from a single piece of Han white marble. It is the most personal of welcomes, yet the choreography underlying the considerate service has been perfected over decades.

Inside is a serene, light-filled lobby, which is the heart of any Peninsula hotel, and a tribute to the Belgravia neighbourhood with its graceful de Gournay landscape murals, elegant, fluted columns, and soaring triple-height carved ceiling adorned with ten sculptural crystal chandeliers. The scene is set for a very British experience—conversations over cups of earthy Pu-erh tea or a classic gin and tonic—in a harmonious blend of East and West.

For Sonja Vodusek, the Managing Director of The Peninsula London at the time of opening, it was important that the hotel continue the traditions of the Hong Kong flagship, which has been regarded as a symbol of cultural exchange for more than a century. "It was among the first to serve English afternoon tea in Hong Kong, British-made Rolls-Royces are synonymous with the hotel's fleet around the world, and even Peninsula hotels' silverware has always been made by a British company. In London, we want to honour our Asian heritage while celebrating and embracing all things British."

Also on the ground floor, Conran and Partners designed The Peninsula Boutique & Café, echoing the Hong Kong flagship's classic Peninsula green, marble, and lacquer interiors, and offering guests and passersby the latest grab-and-go café convenience. And Oriental style takes centre stage at Canton Blue, the glossy Chinese haute cuisine restaurant, which reimagines classic regional dishes with fresh flair. The interiors, conceived by Henry Leung of Hong Kong design studio Cap Atelier, were inspired by the *Keying* junk, a three-masted Chinese trading ship which sailed between China and Britain from 1846 to 1848. "Canton Blue is a dialogue between two cities and cultures that have shared a long history, reflected in the colourful porcelain, reminiscent of what came to Europe on Chinese vessels. We have used these pieces to create feature plate walls, cup screens, and timber wall panels that elegantly frame the dining booths," he explains.

With acclaimed Hong Kong-born chef Dicky To at the culinary helm, Canton Blue juxtaposes Asian and Western worlds, emphasising their deep cross-cultural connection. The cooking is Cantonese-style, but also features the finest British ingredients, so that dishes are likely to include Cornish blue lobster or Herdwick lamb chops—all served on Qing-dynasty-style porcelain, hand-painted in Hong Kong. It's an exotic sensory journey that continues at Little Blue, a cosy bar draped in an abstract ceramic interpretation of bamboo, where cocktails are animated by the spices, fruits, and herbal tinctures of the East. Canton Blue staff ensembles take inspiration from the Ang Lee film *Lust, Caution*, set in Shanghai and Hong Kong in the late 1930s, with brocade dresses, gold lamé high-necked blouses, and stand-collared suits in a sultry midnight blue.

The convergence of cultures continues in The Peninsula London's spacious guest rooms and suites, where details matter and are exact, from the gentle gradation of the palette of ivory to burnished gold and the heft of handsome bronze handles and doors designed to slide away into wall pockets so that they disappear when opened. Hand-tufted carpets by Tai Ping are rich, time-honoured, and contemporary all at once. Sumptuously padded headboards are finished in a delicate silk and hand-

Clockwise from top left: An abstract ceramic interpretation of bamboo in Little Blue; Canton Blue's interiors are inspired by the *Keying* junk, a three-masted Chinese trading ship which sailed between China and Britain from 1846 to 1848; Canton Blue's entrance features ceramic ornamentation; live music played from the music gallery in The Peninsula Hong Kong; Canton Blue's Executive Chef, Dicky To. *Previous pages:* A 1935 Rolls-Royce Phantom II Sedanca de Ville in the hotel courtyard; view of the hotel from The Grand Entrance to Hyde Park.

26

Clockwise from top left: Landscapes painted by Royal Drawing School artists Sarah Lee Roberts (pictured) and Qiong Wu; detail of the Brown Tiger Onyx marble used in The Grand Terrace Suite's powder room; custom-designed textiles in the The Grand Terrace Suite; a Grand Premier Park Room.

embroidered by artisans in Laos. Custom-woven curtains are also decorated by hand, while the shimmering woven wallpaper designed by Peter Marino is made by British-based Fameed Khalique.

Exotic touches include guest bathrooms wrapped in swathes of Turkish honey onyx—perfectly vein-matched in a ripple effect that gives the illusion of being carved out of a single block of stone—and jewel-box-like cabinetry in glass highlighted by glittering accents of gold and silver, handmade by Turkish master craftsman Kerim Kılıçarslan, who also created striking surfaces for The Peninsula Istanbul. It is this synergy of Chinese and European materials and motifs, from delicate Jingdezhen porcelain and fine British bone china to rare Turkish marble and hand-blown glass, that adds distinctive layers to a modern world that acknowledges its past.

L ondon is one of the world's greatest cities, and The Peninsula London is at the very heart of it," says Clement Kwok, Managing Director and Chief Executive Officer of The Hongkong and Shanghai Hotels. As such, the property is an extraordinary homage to the city—every facet, from its architecture and interiors to its impeccable service, celebrates the capital's illustrious history, vibrant culture, and iconic landmarks.

The Lobby is the microcosm of the city. Here guests indulge in the quintessential British tradition of afternoon tea served on bespoke dinnerware designed by Richard Brendon and made by hand in Stoke-on-Trent, and use silver cutlery from William Wright of Sheffield.

Of course the immediate neighbourhood made for the choicest inspiration. More than a physical setting, Belgravia became the main muse for The Peninsula London, with its picturesque crescents, charming garden squares, and parks. The largest of these, Hyde Park, a sweeping 350 acres of serene lakes and magnificent trees, was established in the sixteenth century and served as a guiding light for the murals that grace the hotel's lobby. Meanwhile, the open meadows and mature trees of nearby Green Park and St. James's Park were the influence for Enzo Enea, who says, "The hotel feels like an extension of the surrounding Royal Parks, so when a guest arrives, they already have a sense of being in London." In an extension of that sensation, landscapes painted by artists from the Royal Drawing School, founded by King Charles III and Catherine Goodman in 2000, adorn the guest rooms, suites, and lift lobbies. Even the hotel's bespoke bathroom fragrances, by British-based perfumer Timothy Han—made with natural ingredients and aromatic essences, including shea butter and sweet almond oil—invoke nature.

In keeping with Peninsula tradition, the hotel has a bespoke luxury fleet of British and international cars, including four hybrid Bentley Bentaygas, three electric BMW i7 series, a 1935 vintage Rolls-Royce, two Rolls-Royce Phantoms, an electrified 1960 Austin taxi, and two LEVC London taxis, all finished in Brewster Green. But this is no museum: The entrance driveway has been engineered to accept any supercar in the world, and the hotel's expansive subterranean parking includes an on-site car valet and specialist detailing.

Speaking of automotive excellence, on the rooftop terrace, modern British restaurant and bar Brooklands by Claude Bosi (Brooklands), named in honour of the Surrey racing circuit that is the cradle of British motorsport and aviation, salutes that remarkable legacy with interiors that evoke a Concorde in flight in the dining room, a reflection of the pioneering spirit of British engineering. Brooklands is

also an accolade to the many innovators who have played a part in British history, culture, and sport, brought back to life by David Archer and Julie Humphryes, who have turned a dedicated lift into a whimsical hot air balloon, complete with handwoven wicker and cream leather. "There was a period in post-war history, specifically the 1960s and '70s, when Brooklands was involved in designing parts for the Concorde and contributing to the development of jet engines and supersonic air travel," says Archer. "All of this was happening in Britain, and we wanted Brooklands at the hotel to celebrate that particular moment of technological advancement and craftsmanship." This sense of British heritage is enhanced by a regularly changing display of vintage cars, including the 1933 Napier-Railton, which set and still holds the all-time lap record.

In this inspiring setting, Michelin-starred chef Claude Bosi, Chef Director at Brooklands by Claude Bosi, showcases the diverse produce and cooking styles of the British Isles. "London is all about embracing the new and the different," says Bosi. "As a chef, you don't get to do that in Paris or New York, which is why I love London. Its passion for endless variety and diversity makes it incredibly exciting." His menu features locally sourced seasonal ingredients such as Dorset crabs, Scottish razor clams, and cep mushrooms, while the bar serves MACH II gin, specially distilled for the hotel by the Cambridge Distillery.

Another highlight of Brooklands is The Tabac, with a humidor that holds up to two thousand cigars, making it a must for cigar connoisseurs. Its mahogany-and-brass interiors, and cabinets lined with Okoume wood from West Africa, are influenced by the timber bodywork and chassis of the iconic Brooklands racing cars.

Fashion designer Jenny Packham also drew on a distinctly British vocabulary to expand the story of The Peninsula London through the wardrobe she created for more than five hundred team

members of the hotel, whom Packham calls "the living embodiment of the power of British style." The concept draws on legendary figures such as Michael Caine, Julie Christie, and Charlotte Rampling, as well as traditional Asian designs, crafted in impeccably tailored, fluid silhouettes in neutral and jewel-like hues. The entire wardrobe reflects The Peninsula's commitment to quality and style for all—from the bell service to the staff operating behind the scenes—a bold blend of sophistication and simplicity. The chic '60s monochromatic colour scheme, contemporary sculpted shoulder lines and cinched waists, sharply tailored suits, and satin crepe dresses in shades of champagne and claret mirror the rich tones and textures of the interiors and elegant murals. Brooklands' smart suits in Air Force blue for men and, for women, sky-blue skirt suits with Concorde-inspired belt buckles call to mind the futuristic allure and liberated spirit of the supersonic aircraft.

As you turn the pages of this story, dear traveller, you will find yourself at the heart of all we do. Here, every guest takes centre stage, and London becomes the ever-changing backdrop to your adventures.

As you wander through the city's bustling streets, you will discover that The Peninsula London is not just a hotel: It is your steadfast companion as you explore the city's hidden corners, uncover its secrets, and immerse yourself in its rich history. Together we will weave a tapestry of memories, filled with twists and turns and delightful surprises, creating a vibrant reflection of a life well-lived, infused with joy, integrity, adventure, and respect.

Brooklands, c. 1930s. *Pages 32-35:* The Peninsula London's courtyard with the 120-year-old maple trees in the centre.

66 For us, the guest is everything. Our entire philosophy is about creating a 'home away from home' where true luxury is a proud culture of service that means you want to come back. **99**

The Hon. Sir Michael Kadoorie
Chairman, The Hongkong and Shanghai Hotels, Limited

Artwork by Kevin Harman in The Reception. *Opposite:* The Reception. *Following pages:* Landscape painted by artist Douglas Farthing from the Royal Drawing School; The Reception. *Pages 50-51:* A lift to the guest rooms and suites; a Peninsula Page in The Lobby. *Pages 52-53:* The Peninsula Suite overlooking Hyde Park Corner includes a private gym and screening room and a dedicated lift.

"The most important thing is how it makes them feel. You always have an emotional response to the interiors of a building. It's a little bit like us—we all have rich inner lives.**"**

Peter Marino
Architect and Designer of the Interiors

The Arch Suite. *Previous pages:* A premier guest room; Wellington Arch seen from The Arch Suite. *Following pages:* Detail of a Peter Marino-designed headboard. *Page 60:* Grand Premier Park guest room. *Page 61, clockwise from top left:* A Peter Marino-designed curtain; illustration of a Grand Premier Park guest room; in-room technology includes personal tablets pre-set in eleven languages and touch-screen controls for light, temperature, and privacy.

57

> 66 Few places
> do service
> and technology
> like this. And
> there aren't many
> London locations
> that feel quite
> as rarefied. 99

Condé Nast Traveller

" Peninsula team members are the living embodiment of the power of British style. "

Jenny Packham
Wardrobe Designer

British fashion designer Jenny Packham designed The Peninsula London staff wardrobe. *Previous pages:* The Arch Suite, with interiors inspired by quintessentially British residences, offers uninterrupted views of its namesake—the iconic Wellington Arch. *Following pages:* The hotel's staff wardrobe draws on legendary British figures such as Michael Caine, Julie Christie, and Charlotte Rampling, as well as traditional Asian designs. *Pages 68-69:* Brooklands' staff wardrobe takes inspiration from the design of the Concorde; The Lobby staff wardrobe in rich claret.

A Day in the Life

As the newest of The Peninsula Hotels, London is the youngest member of a family known for refinement, elegance, and adventure. There are shared family traits, but each individual property is unique, and The Peninsula London is ready to make its own mark.

As the doors of The Peninsula London swing open, you are greeted with a chorus of warm welcomes. It's early morning and the city is already humming with life, yet tranquillity prevails. In The Lobby, tables are laden with breakfast, from English muffins topped with poached eggs to servings of plump dim sum, and silver pots of tea are steaming. The day is just beginning.

The luggage has already been delivered to your suite, an inviting haven overlooking Wellington Arch. A large plush armchair, strategically placed by the window, beckons you to pause, to sit and read, or simply to watch the world go by—a retreat from the fray, yet a window seat that misses none of the action. The valet box is at your disposal, as is the latest in-room technology. The staff, attentive to your preferences, have added extra pillows and your favourite fresh cut flowers, adjusting the room's temperature and lighting till it is just so.

The inviting indoor twenty-five-metre pool calls for a brisk morning swim, but first, stop by the concierge desk to inquire about tickets for a must-see, sold-out musical. London's famed theatre district is just a stroll away.

After a swim, a massage at the spa is too tempting to resist. Refreshed, and armed with a new supply of lotions and potions, indulge in a piping hot chocolate and delicious pastries in the sunshine at The Peninsula Boutique & Café. Afterwards, a little shopping in the hotel's elegant colonnade of boutiques facing Wellington Arch.

Then explore the city, losing yourself in its history, its culture, its charm. A leisurely walk through nearby Green Park, past Buckingham Palace to St. James's Park, invigorates. The park's lake is home to pelicans, their forefathers a gift to Charles II in 1664. Continue as far as Mayfair, and then, on your return, enjoy an art exhibition at the Serpentine Galleries in Kensington Gardens.

Afternoon tea in The Lobby is a feast of delicate finger sandwiches, freshly baked scones topped with raspberry and mint jam, and endless cups of tea, a delightful way to while away the time, perhaps with a book on London's formal gardens or the latest Booker Prize winner.

As evening falls, before dinner at Brooklands by Claude Bosi, there are cocktails—whether an espresso martini or classic gin and tonic—with friends. Dine under the gleaming fuselage of the Concorde, a spectacular celebration of human ingenuity, with the glittering London landscape stretching into the distance.

The evening ends with drinks at Little Blue—and a mental note to return the next day for Peking duck and black truffle tofu at Canton Blue. Back in your suite, the curtains drawn, the lamps lit, a bath awaits, infused with the hotel's signature organic fragrance imbued with British wildflowers. Then drift off to sleep looking forward to another day, content to simply be back at The Peninsula London.

" It is our employees who each and every day are the ones who offer an exceptional guest experience, providing a genuine connection and insight into London. "

Peter Borer
Chief Operating Officer, The Hongkong and Shanghai Hotels, Limited

Opposite: A Peninsula Page shows a guest Big Ben. *Pages 72-75:* Scenes from London, including Belgravia, Regent Street, and Tower Bridge over the River Thames. *Following pages:* Young Peninsula guests sightseeing outside Buckingham Palace in an automobile from the hotel's famed fleet.

The Serpentine, a sixteen-hectare lake in Hyde Park, was created in 1730. Guests can visit the park on bespoke Peninsula Pashley Cycles. *Opposite:* Hyde Park is outside the hotel's doors.
Following pages: Wellington Arch in Belgravia can be seen from several of the guest rooms; the hotel is in the vibrant centre of London's Belgravia neighbourhood.

> **"The Peninsula London has been three decades in the making, and casts the capital in a glamorous, magical light."**
>
> *The Times*

A custom-fabricated wicker and leather-lined lift to Brooklands designed by Archer Humphryes Architects; the restaurant and bar has its own dedicated lifts. *Opposite:* Brooklands' ground-floor lift lobby. *Following pages:* Napier Railton private dining room, Brooklands.

The Brooklands Bar interior references the legendary Brooklands racing circuit in Surrey, the birthplace of British motor racing sport and flight innovation. The Napier Railton Lounge (*above*) was designed to emulate the body of the 1933 Napier-Railton, a racing car that holds the lap speed record at Brooklands racing circuit. *Opposite:* A thirteen-and-a-half-metre-long model of the iconic Concorde aircraft is suspended from the ceiling of Brooklands' dining room. *Following pages:* To continue the theme, the restaurant has Concorde-inspired napkin holders.

66 London is all about embracing the new and the different.... Its passion for endless variety and diversity makes it incredibly exciting. 99

Claude Bosi
Chef Director, Brooklands by Claude Bosi

The terrace at Brooklands has spectacular panoramic views over London.
Opposite: The restaurant's Mach II private dining room. *Previous pages:* Michelin-starred chef Claude Bosi (pictured),
Chef Director of Brooklands, showcases the diverse produce and cooking styles
of the British Isles. *Pages 102-7:* The Brooklands terrace is the perfect spot to host glamorous happenings.

66 There was a period in post-war history, specifically the 1960s and '70s, when Brooklands was involved in designing parts for the Concorde and contributing to the development of supersonic air travel. All of this was happening in Britain, and we wanted Brooklands to celebrate that particular moment of technological advancement and craftsmanship. 99

David Archer
Brooklands by Claude Bosi, Architect

At Brooklands Bar, the intricate latticed ceiling is inspired by the geodetic construction of the Vickers Wellington bomber designed in the 1930s. *Previous pages:* The entrance to Brooklands features a custom inlay work of art that pays homage to the Brooklands motor-racing circuit in Surrey. *Pages 108-11:* The mahogany-panelled Tasting Room cigar lounge. *Following pages:* Brooklands Bar offers an unparalleled nighttime view over London's iconic skyline, from St. Paul's to Big Ben.

Opposite: The deep leather banquette seating is a replica of the seating in the Rolls-Royce Silver Ghost. *Following pages:* Brooklands Bar. 119

Conceptual cocktails at Brooklands Bar. *Opposite:* Further playing up the theme of British aviation and motorsports, the bar's dazzling crystal chandelier replicates the blades of a Rolls-Royce turbine jet engine. *Following pages:* The dramatic staircase leading to the St. George Ballroom makes for a grand entrance. *Page 127:* A vintage 1935 Rolls-Royce Phantom II Sedanca de Ville in the hotel's courtyard.

The Peninsula Spa and Wellness Centre. *Opposite:* The walls of the hotel's twenty-five-metre swimming pool are adorned with an intricate mosaic depicting a tranquil landscape. The illuminated overhead light panels change throughout the course of the day to simulate natural sunlight. *Previous pages:* Bathrooms are wrapped in swathes of perfectly matched Turkish honey onyx to create a ripple effect. *Pages 136-41:* Featuring street-level window displays and an alfresco terrace, The Peninsula Boutique & Café offers coffee, patisserie, all-day light lunches, and signature branded products and fine gifts.

> **"** The hotel feels like an extension of the surrounding Royal Parks, so when a guest arrives, they already have a sense of being in London. **"**

Enzo Enea
Landscape Architect, The Peninsula London

Opposite: Physical Energy, a bronze equestrian sculpture by British artist George Frederic Watts (1817-1904), is located near the juncture of Hyde Park and Kensington Gardens. *Previous pages:* The Peninsula London's four-legged friends enjoy pet-sitting and walking services, plush beds, customised feeding bowls, tailored menus, and delicious treats; The Peninsula London's Senior Gardener, Bryanne Melville. *Following pages:* The Royal Albert Hall, the concert hall on the northern edge of South Kensington, was opened by Queen Victoria in 1871.

66 The back of house of a hotel is just as important as the front of house. We want to ensure that our team members feel good about where they work. This creates a solid team spirit and enhances our colleagues' ability to deliver the highest quality of service to our guests. 99

Peter Borer

The Peninsula London welcomes domestic pets, emotional-support animals, and service animals.
Opposite: The hotel's Portland-stone façade. *Previous pages:* A photo of the iconic Peninsula Pages. In the background
is a landscape painting by Fraser Scarfe, a graduate of the Royal Drawing School. He is one of more than
forty British artists from the Royal Drawing School whose works are displayed in the hotel.

" What Peter Marino brought was what we requested, and that was a lightness that is not necessarily traditional in London. He brought in, for an international guest, a certain levity. We did not want to be another traditional London hotel. "

The Hon. Sir Michael Kadoorie

The Peninsula London also includes twenty-five private residences designed under the direction of Peter Marino.
Following pages: Amenities at The Peninsula Residences London include a private, twenty-five-metre indoor swimming pool.

The hotel's ground-floor shopping arcade hosts nine luxury boutiques, including the London flagship of high jeweller and watchmaker Mouawad. *Opposite:* The arcade is also home to iconic British luxury house Asprey, which chose The Peninsula for its second boutique in London. *Following pages:* Inside Mouawad's opulent boutique. *Pages 162-63:* All of the hotel's guest rooms feature mahogany-panelled dressing rooms. *Pages 164-65:* The hotel's private screening room takes cues from classic British cinema and boasts Dolby surround sound, a two-hundred-inch micro-perforated viewing screen, and a 1950s 70mm film projector.

159

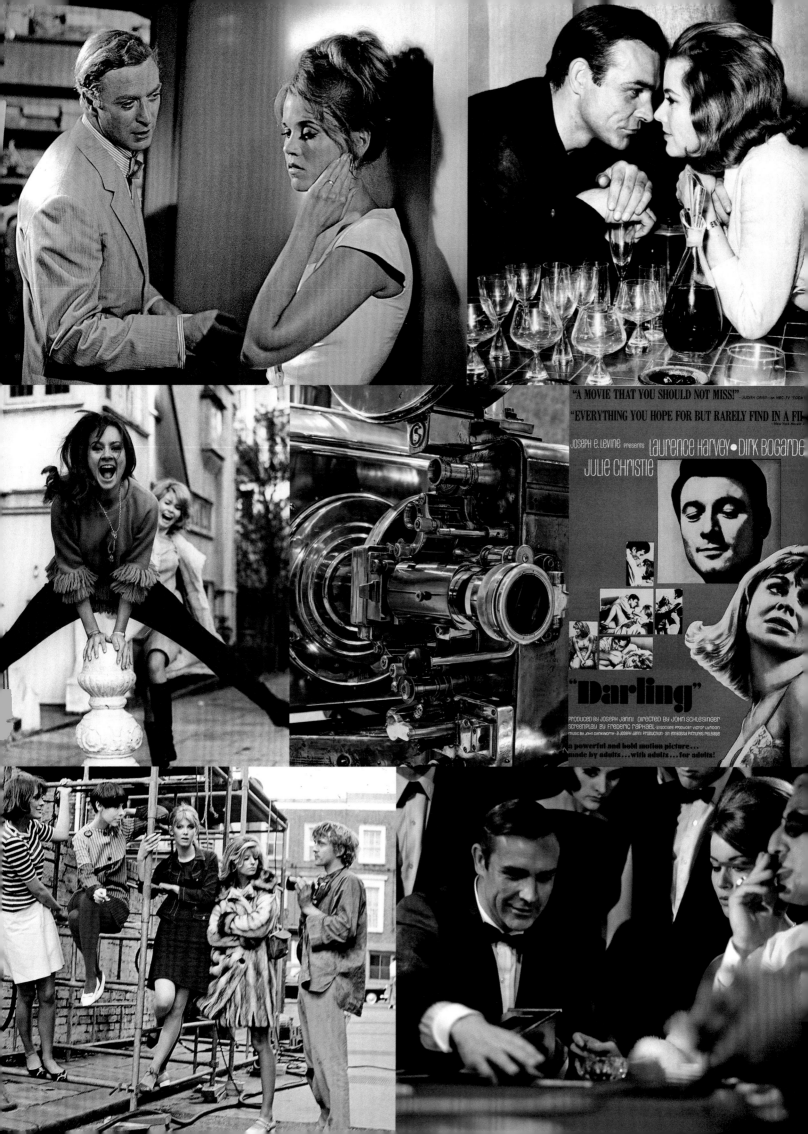

The street-level entrance to Little Blue cocktail bar is flanked by stone lions. *Opposite:* Little Blue, whose décor reflects both British and Chinese history, has classic leather seats, etched glass, and a wall of apothecary-style spice cabinets. *Previous pages:* Little Blue. *Page 166:* The Tasting Room cigar lounge, overseen by Master of Havana Cigars Manu Harit, has a walk-in humidor and a collection of rare whiskies. *Page 167:* An interior detail of The Silk Room, one of Canton Blue's two private dining rooms. *Following pages:* Canton Blue's interiors were inspired by the *Keying* junk, a three-masted Chinese trading ship which sailed between China and Britain from 1846 to 1848; Little Blue's cocktails are animated by the spices, fruits, and herbal tinctures of the East; the Little Blue lobby. 171

> 66 London is one of the world's greatest cities, and The Peninsula London is at the very heart of it. 99

Clement Kwok
Managing Director and Chief Executive Officer,
The Hongkong and Shanghai Hotels, Limited

Canton Blue's menu incorporates fresh British produce, such as Cornish blue lobster, here braised with aged Cheddar, Stilton, girolles, and rice cakes. *Opposite:* Dim sum at Canton Blue. *Previous pages:* The main dining room at Canton Blue. *Pages 176-77:* The Music Room at Canton Blue. *Pages 174-75:* Canton Blue.

"Canton Blue is a dialogue between two cities and cultures that have shared a long history, reflected in the colourful porcelain, reminiscent of what came to Europe on Chinese vessels. We have used these pieces to create plate walls, cup screens, and timber wall panels that elegantly frame the dining booths."

Henry Leung
Interior Designer, Canton Blue

Opposite: Intricate display panels of colourful Cantonese porcelain frame Canton Blue's dining booths.
Previous pages: The restaurant's Tea Lounge, with a gilded caisson ceiling inspired by the grandeur of the Forbidden City in Beijing during the Ming dynasty. *Following page:* The Lobby's music gallery. *Pages 187-89:* The Lobby's triple-height, intricately moulded ceilings and hand-blown crystal chandeliers.

The Peninsula London's opening day ceremony, on September 12, 2023, featured live music.
Opposite: The Peninsula London hosted the 2024 BAFTA Gala. *Following pages and page 195:* The hotel's Colleague
Christmas Party in 2023. *Page 194:* Sir Rod Stewart performs onstage at the 2024 Prince's Trust "Invest in Futures"
gala held in the St. George Ballroom at The Peninsula London. *Pages 196-97:* Olivia Dean and Michael Ward
at the hotel the night of the 2023 Fashion Awards. *Pages 198-99:* Zara McDermott before the Fashion Awards;
the hotel maintains a fleet of custom vehicles for the convenience of guests. *Pages 200-201:* The 2023 Brooklands New
Year's Eve party offered attendees a spectacular front-row seat to London's fireworks.

"I had been looking for the right location for thirty-five years. Now it's time to celebrate."

The Hon. Sir Michael Kadoorie

Acknowledgements

I still remember my first visit to The Peninsula Hong Kong. It was more than three decades ago, but the experience remains etched in my memory. The Grande Dame was—and is still—quintessential Hong Kong, a wonderful expression of heritage and innovation all at once. Since then, I have had the immense pleasure of staying at Peninsula hotels around the world, from Paris and Tokyo to New York and Istanbul, and so I feel especially honoured to author this book on The Peninsula London, and to be a small part of a unique legacy of hospitality that has stood the test of time and distance.

First and foremost, I would like to express my deepest gratitude to Sir Michael Kadoorie. His vision and devotion to excellence are at the heart of every Peninsula hotel's legendary hospitality.

I would also like to extend my sincere thanks to The Hongkong and Shanghai Hotels, and to Chief Executive Officer Clement Kwok and Chief Operating Officer Peter Borer, who both provided fascinating insights into the thirty-five years that have led up to the London hotel.

I am indebted to Carson Glover for his enlightened direction, and to his dedicated marketing team, including Liz Healey, Jona Puentespina, and Leela Rose. I am especially grateful to Rolf Buehlmann and Sonja Vodusek, along with Ming Chen, Alastair Keeble, John Miller, James Overbaugh, Gareth Roberts, Vicky Sharman-Cox, Florian Thireau, and Susan Wheatley for their accumulated wisdom. And special thanks to Lynne Mulholland for her invaluable advice, and to Clare Wadsworth for her meticulous eye and editing skills.

My heartfelt thanks to the Poet Laureate Simon Armitage for making this book unique, and to Peter Marino for spending the time with me to discuss his peerless creative inspiration. I would like to express my appreciation, too, to everyone who has contributed, in particular architects David Archer and Julie Humphryes, chefs Claude Bosi and Dicky To, illustrators Lydia Bourhill and Caroline Tomlinson, landscape architect Enzo Enea, Jim Greaves and Mike Taylor of Hopkins Architects, interior designer Henry Leung, Conran and Partners' Tina Norden, fashion designer Jenny Packham, and Fraser Scarfe and the other artists of the Royal Drawing School.

I would also like to acknowledge Martine and Prosper Assouline. I am beholden to Kristian Laliberte for expertly and patiently guiding the publishing process, and to his expert editorial team, above all Kirsten Chilstrom, Andrea Ramirez, Jihyun Kim, and Bobbie Richardson. Your passion for creating beautiful books is truly exhilarating.

Lastly, my eternal gratitude to my husband, Alistair Gough, for his unwavering support, patience, and insightful contributions throughout this project.

—Catherine Shaw

ABOUT THE AUTHOR

Catherine Shaw is a leading writer, editor, and consultant specialising in architecture and design. She has written and contributed to over ten books, including award-winning monographs on art collector and designer Alan Chan and on architect William Lim's Asian design philosophy. She has also authored books on architect André Fu, on Turkish interior designer Zeynep Fadıllıoğlu, and on Beijing-based OPEN Architecture's most significant cultural projects across China. An international design consultant with master's degrees in urban and environmental planning, Shaw also advises on design trends and is a regular speaker and moderator at design events such as Milan Design Week and Art Basel Hong Kong. She is the Asia-Pacific contributing editor for *Metropolis,* and divides her time between Hong Kong and London.

CREDITS

All images © Oliver Pilcher, except:
Pages 4-5: © Jason Hawkes Photography; pp. 6-7: © Caroline Tomlinson; p. 8 (clockwise from top left): © Francisco Guerrero, © HSH, © Benjamin McMahon, © HSH; pp. 10-11, 15, 36, 70, 81, 114, 119, 145, 153, 172, 185, 202-203: © Lydia Bourhill/@bourhillustration; pp. 12-13, 34-35, 40, 42-43, 46, 47, 50, 51, 54, 60, 62-63, 88, 90-91, 96-97, 104-105, 112-113, 116-117, 132-133, 134, 136-137, 162-163, 170, 171, 178-179: © Will Pryce; p. 16 (clockwise from top left): © HSH, © Peninsula, © HSH, © HSH, © Oliver Jones, © HSH; p. 19 (clockwise from top left): © Lisa Tse, © Hopkins Architects, © Francisco Guerrero; pp. 20-21, 86-87: © Oliver Jones; p. 22 (top row): © Oliver Pilcher, © Peninsula, © Oliver Pilcher; (middle row): © Oliver Pilcher, © Peter Marino, © Oliver Jones; (bottom row, all): © Oliver Pilcher; p. 27 (clockwise from top left): © Oliver Pilcher, All Rights Reserved, © Peninsula, © HSH, © Lisa Tse; p. 28 (clockwise from top left): © Alecsandra Dragoi, © Alecsandra Dragoi, © Peninsula, © Peninsula, © Peninsula, © Will Pryce; pp. 30-31: Brooklands Museum; pp. 32-33: © Ben Hoy Slot; p. 37: Luggage by Globe Trotter Luggage; p. 44: © Milo Brown; pp. 38-39: Accessories by Aspinal of London; p. 48: © Royal Drawing School, Douglas Farthings; pp. 52-53: © Jonathan Bond; p. 56: Menswear by Oliver Brown; pp. 58, 59, 98 (bottom left), 135, 200-201: © Peninsula; p. 61 (clockwise from top left): © Peninsula, © Lydia Bourhill/@bourhillustration, © Will Pryce; pp. 64, 66, 67, 69 (bottom): © Alecsandra Dragoi; pp. 69 (top), 190, 192-193, 195: © Lisa Tse; pp. 72, 73, 74-75, 144, 148-149: © Francisco Guerrero; pp. 76, 78-79: © Sam Wild; p. 83: Accessories by Aspinal of London, Menswear by Oliver Brown; pp. 89, 93, 95, 100, 123, 155, 156-157, 164: © Taran Wilkhu; pp. 92, 98 (top row), 99, 118, 122: © Sam Harris; p. 101: Menswear by Oliver Brown; pp. 102-103: Womenswear by Jenny Packham, Accessories by Boodles, Menswear by Oliver Brown; pp. 124-125: Womenswear by Jenny Packham, Accessories by Boodles; p. 139: © Adrianna Giakoumis; p. 141: Accessories by Aspinal of London, Menswear by Oliver Brown; p. 142: Accessories by BagButler; p. 151: © Royal Drawing School, Fraser Scarfe; pp. 158: © Josep Serveto Estefanell; p. 159: © Ellie Pinney; p. 165 (clockwise from top left): © Sunset Boulevard/Corbis via Getty Images, © Bettmann/Getty Images, © Everett Collection, © Mario De Biasi/Mondadori via Getty Images, © Everett Collection, © RGR Collection/Alamy Stock Photo; pp. 172, 173, 176-177, 180, 181, 182-183: © Eleonora Boscarelli; p. 184: Menswear by Oliver Brown; p. 191: BAFTA via Getty Images; p. 194: © Dave Benett/Getty Images; pp. 196, 197, 198: © Seye Isikalu/Courtesy of the British Fashion Council; p. 199: Dress by Jenny Packham.

The publisher would like to thank the following: Julien Marnier, British Fashion Council; Marie-Claire Westover, Lipstick of London; The Hon. Isobel Kershaw, The Stylist London.

Every possible effort has been made to identify and contact all rights holders and obtain their permission for work appearing in these pages. Any errors or omissions brought to the publisher's attention will be corrected in future editions.

Front and back cover: © Oliver Pilcher

© 2024 Assouline Publishing
3 Park Avenue, 27th Floor
New York, NY 10016, USA
Tel: 212 989-6769   Fax: 212 647-0005

Editor: Kristian Laliberte
Creative director: Jihyun Kim
Art director: Bobbie Richardson
Photo editor: Kirsten Chilstrom

ISBN: 9781649802446
Printed in Italy by Grafiche Milani.

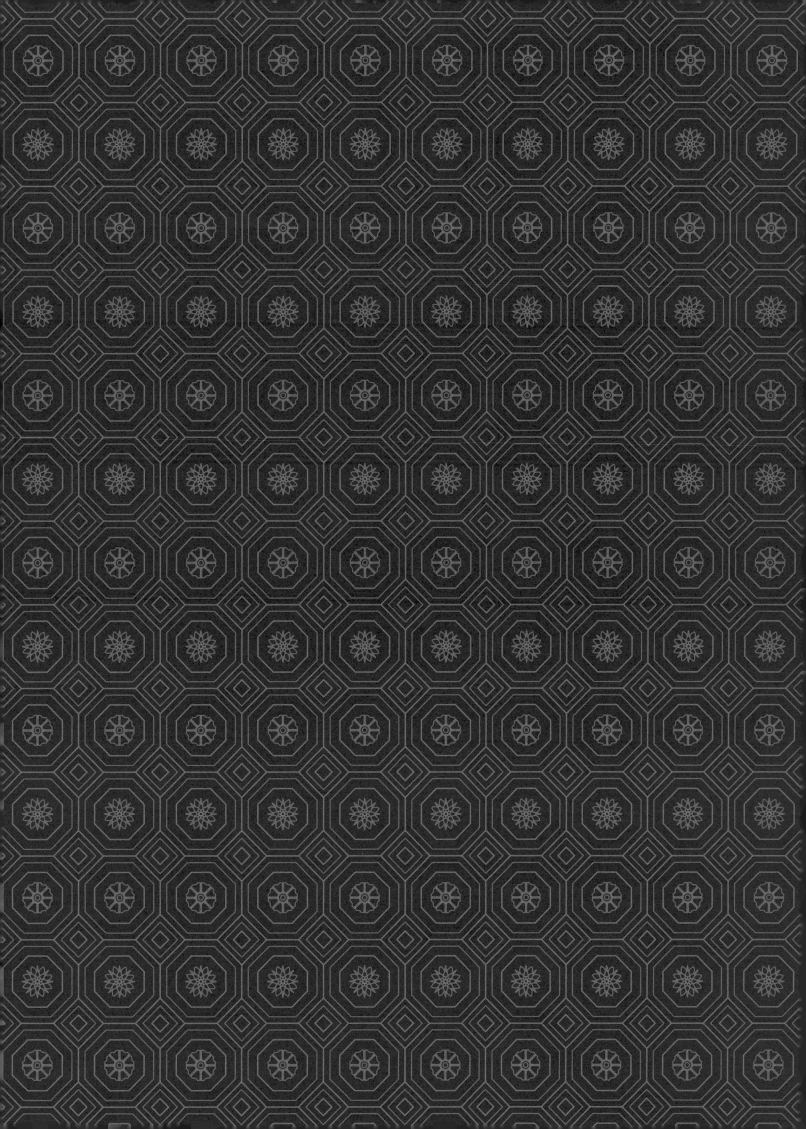

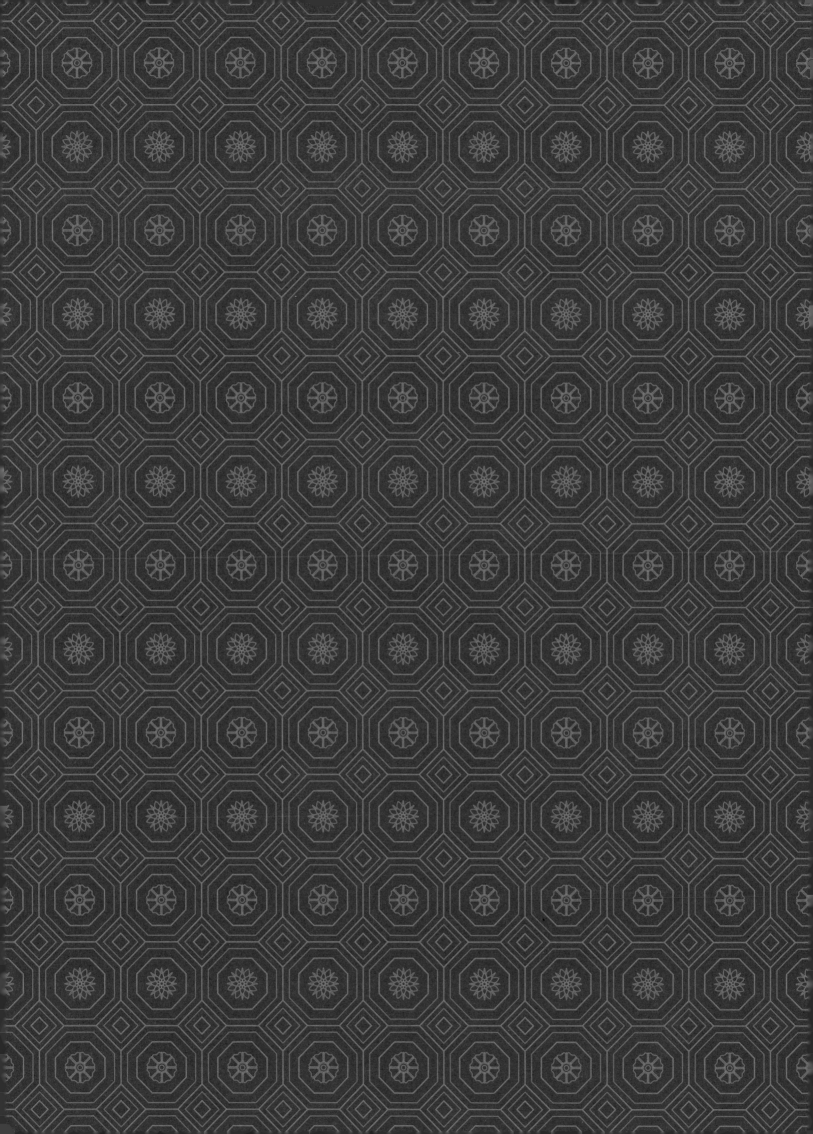